#ChampTalk

An inspiring & thought-provoking collection of lessons unpacked through authentic quotes.

C.L. Whiteside
@ChampionLife23

Contents

Introduction

The Making of #ChampTalk

The purpose of this book is to share best practices that will enable people to be conscious of the choices they make, mindful of the thoughts they think, attuned to the emotions they feel, and aware of the environment they create. The concept of #*ChampTalk* stems from my fascination with quotes. I love quotes because they can be memorized and drawn upon easily. Each section of this book begins with a quote I created in response to valuable experiences I have encountered as a teacher, coach, athlete, son, brother, uncle, friend, mentor, and child of God. Lessons can be simplified into a single quote, which immortalizes the valuable principles built into any meaningful teaching. Though the purpose of this book isn't to convert anyone spiritually, it will include lessons from the Bible. The Bible is the place many of my thoughts, philosophies, and principles are rooted in. All of my experiences and endeavors have not been triumphant. Nonetheless, they have all been useful. The wide range of views and convictions stem from my backstory and diverse background. My history within education and athletics has allowed me to distinguish many different walks of life—from living in the affluent and luxurious Hamptons (Long Island, New York) and seeing firsthand that a perfect life on the surface doesn't guarantee contentment and happiness to seeing there is hope even in the worst neighborhoods. The connections I have made throughout my adventures have given me the opportunity to discern the wins, losses, and paths taken from athletes who made it big professionally to athletes who would love to have a second opportunity, to individuals who are extremely wise in business and great with money, to individuals who would have a PhD in "street smarts" (if there was such a thing) and could sell sand to the beach. The widespread spectrum of mentalities and paths of life I have been exposed to make me grateful and have illuminated what really matters in life. Through my observations, relationships, and reflections, I understand better than ever that our successes don't define us and our failures don't kill us, but our beliefs do carry us. My quotes are pearls of wisdom built upon personal truths and experiences. Even so, the beauty of quotes is they may be interpreted in a manner which fits your story, allowing you to draw upon past experiences or become aware of personal ambitions. *As you start each selection, take a moment to see how the quote resonates with you personally. At the end of each selection there are opportunities to reflect and put into practice what is discussed. You may feel comfortable doing this in a journal, directly taking notes in your book, or highlighting portions you connected with most. Active reflecting allows for a more in-depth and better reading experience.*

Author's Note

My State of Change

I've found I'm constantly studying my failures.

I've noticed I'm conscious of my flaws and know my errors.

I've embraced and am aware of my mistakes, so I can accept them and not break.

I regret some things which would make most battle with their belief in fate.

I strive for change, and it can just be half a dime.

The more change there is, however, doesn't mean it'll all add up over time.

Likewise, if I could do some things over I'd be a fool to have repeated crimes.

Though progress has always come from change,

Change doesn't necessarily mean progress is the gain.

Progress is what I live for, and today it's the focus of my pain.

If your attention is not on getting better, then your intentions can only be on getting worse.

So, though I no longer need to be the best to all or the John Wooden of this game,

I see the importance of understanding one's self is enough to fulfill a man's name.

Every second is a present, while the present is always a product of a past move.

So, every day is a battle with the present because it shapes my future and my will to improve.

Though I no longer wish to be the one to give my best to all—

I battle, and I wish to give all my best to ONE.

It is true.

#ChampTalk

Many want a specific type of life, love, or peace but fail to realize half of knowing what you want is knowing what you must give up to get it.

#ChampTalk

Being wise is not about having a lot of knowledge. Being wise is about having knowledge and knowing how to apply it effectively.

#ChampTalk

If your attention is not on getting better, then your intentions are to get worse.

"The grass always looks greener on the other side, but instead of moving, I've decided to water my lawn." #ChampTalk

Is the Grass Greener?

Do you ever find yourself complaining about what you don't have and can easily point out why so-and-so has it so much easier and better? We all do this from time to time. When we do this, we are the person sitting on the porch, looking to the other side, thinking "I wish my grass would get that green, but I don't have a big tree for shade like they do." Why does the grass look greener on the other side? Our vision can be altered because of the angle we are looking at it from, or the grass on the other side is actually greener. Having said that, every so often we are too busy paying attention to everyone else's lawn, to the point that we don't realize our lawn is just as green or greener. Despite that, if we are focusing and giving our all to our own lawn, it would be quite difficult to notice what is going on with anyone else's lawn.

We can complain and grumble, water it, make time to plant a tree for shade, or come up with another innovative way to improve our lawn. Likewise, caution even needs to be taken when admiring another lawn, so we don't become envious. When it comes down to it, you can always find someone who you "think" has it better off than you in one regard or another. They have more material possessions, more money, or a so

1

called better life. A person might have one of the most beautiful and largest homes you have ever seen and you would do anything to trade places with them since you can't see the husband and wife are in the middle of a divorce, the mother has cancer, or the husband just got laid off. There are tons of situations where people make drastic changes since they feel *the grass looks greener on the other side*. Some would include: transferring schools, switching jobs, ending a relationship to pursue a new one, changing teams, and relocating just to name a few. Different opportunities don't always mean better, commonly they just mean DIFFERENT.

If we're always looking and counting what others have, we will never realize the blessings we've received. Instead of getting consumed with what others have, one should take the necessary steps to improve his or her lawn. If you have done all you can and still believe the lawn looks better—then by all means, make the switch. Remember this: the best way to get what you want is to be grateful for what you have already and to always seek the positive, not the negative. When we stop comparing and reflect, sometimes we notice we have roses growing in our lawn that we never even noticed before. No matter what though—before making that move to the other side—take time out to water your lawn, and see what happens.

1. Think about 5 things you are grateful for in your life. How can you make those things even better?
2. Think about 3 different ways you want your life to improve. Give 3 steps for each improvement you can make better.

"You can tell a man to be a King, but if he's only seen soldiers then a soldier is what he will become since that's all he knows." #ChampTalk

Trained Soldier

When examining a king or queen's upbringing in history, we see they were exposed and taught by the best in the kingdom. Similarly, I had a kingdom to raise me into the man I am. I have had parents, family-friends, pastors, barbers, coaches, and teachers guide me along the way. I appreciate those who share a passion and bring others along their journey with them. I had a family-friend who loved sports and trading cards and would take me to sports memorabilia stores with him. During our road trips, the car rides allowed him to share knowledge about everything from basketball cards to women. Correspondingly, I understand how to prepare for speaking engagements because my pastor had me read scripture lessons in front of the church congregation. I also had a forensics instructor who showed me the proper way to get ready and practice when I was in grade school. In similar fashion, I recognize the effects of serving others since I had an admissions counselor in college who took time to listen, to see how I was doing, and to check up on me, which he still does to this day. In like manner, I see the importance of paying attention to detail, having observed my coaches work and working under them at camps. I was exposed to many different idiosyncratic and awesome characteristics. I relished these characteristics and copied those best I could because of these different people in my life. To add to this, if people see greatness, awesome work ethic, good manners, genuine communication, and authentic perseverance on a regular basis more than not, they, like all children, emulate what they see. Before you know it, what you emulate becomes habit.

Being a black male raised in the ruthless city of Milwaukee, where so many black males have been consumed by the streets, I have had so many people ask and wonder, "How did I make it?" My answer isn't complicated. My father made it, so I was setup to make it. I cannot try to boast and say I was some intrinsically unique person because I had two parents who taught me and showed me the way. My dad earning a Master's degree gave me a conviction I would graduate high school and college in view of the fact that there was a legacy and tradition in my life of "this is what you're supposed to do."

Many people wonder why others don't make it. The cycle of not making it is repetitive and endless, unless one of two things happen. First, a soldier seeks people from a different lifestyle to teach him the path of royalty. The first part starts with realizing and admitting we can use a helping hand. We have to remind ourselves everyone has gotten help and guidance at some point, so we can't be too prideful. Seeking teams, boards, and organizations are key since they have people we can learn from. We should research, observe, get involved, and talk to others with listening ears. This can be uncomfortable but is essential. The second way happens when those within the kingdom find others to mentor and show them they can be more than just troopers. Both parties are important; although the most important side is the soldiers. In spite of that, soldiers who don't immerse themselves in the learning process, refuse counsel, and have hardened their hearts will fall victim to the toxic cycle. My dad, who did not have his father and was raised by a single mother on welfare, had to seek guidance from teachers, counselors, and coaches. His dream would have been to play on his school's basketball team, but that didn't work out. It would have been easy and understandable for him to stop here since his dream was taken away, but he realized he still needed to be a part of something. I've seen too many rob themselves of opportunities to grow because they didn't make a team or have a situation play out like they had hoped. When one door closes, some don't even bother to try another. My father didn't give up. He realized there were other doors to try; he took a chance and joined the cross country team and started taking martial arts classes. A simple move like this gave him coaches and people to look out for him. Additionally, he made sure to watch those he knew were considered successful in a particular aspect and study their 'how.' He made sure to have conversations with teachers and professors and listen to their constructive criticism. At best, he was supposed to become a soldier and another statistic. My father realized he had to seek past what his eyes could see.

Not only do we need more soldiers to strive to be kings and queens, we need more kings, queens, and kingdoms willing to show soldiers there are opportunities and paths they can take that they may have otherwise never realized existed. You can't have one without the other, and—if you're like me and blessed to have a village to raise you—don't forget this and become arrogant and act like it was ALL you. We were lucky, so give back. If you were like my father and not so lucky, know you CAN'T do it all by yourself. A great part of the reason why I chose the profession of teaching and coaching is because it gives me an abundant amount of opportunities to give back and to be a mentor.

5

Whether it's playing 1 on 1 (basketball), encouraging students to join or apply for organizations and school trips, taking athletes home or to church, listening and discussing different issues, or tutoring or training students after hours—I've been blessed to have chances to give back with fairly good reception. This is only possible because I'm willing to share, be vulnerable, and admit my mistakes. I don't try and put myself on a pedestal and say, "Since I made it, why can't you?" I admit to them how much help I've had during my life. I stress to my athletes and students the importance of having mentors and people who look out for you. No one, no matter what they think, has ever done it by themselves. There are so many paths to learn the way of royalty, and more often than not, people who are even willing to show you the way.

1. List at least 5 mentors or people you can go to for wise counsel. List at least 1 reason you can find counsel in each of the people you've listed.
2. List 3 ways you can mentor someone. Think about your strengths, passions, and opportunities that make you unique.
3. List three people you mentor and a reason why you mentor them. If you don't mentor anyone, identify 3 people you can mentor and why. It's okay to target someone with a similar passion or interest and someone who is easily accessible. In fact, I would encourage this if you are first starting off.

"You can only know what's shaping your thoughts when you know what you're feeding your mind." #ChampTalk

Thoughts Feed the Mind

Garbage in equals garbage out. Everything we see, do, and hear has some impact on us, whether we would like to admit this or not. I preach this to my students and athletes all the time. The young woman who watches tons of Instagram videos and reality TV shows promoting sex, partying, and confrontation is influenced. She claims it has no effect on her, but she has failed to notice she wants to dress in skimpier clothes, screams and yells when she has a disagreement, and aims to be seen and not respected. Then you have the young man who is influenced because he listens to music about violence and watches YouTube videos of people being knocked out. He claims he just likes the beats of the songs but doesn't realize how much more he swears and curses or how he aims to act tough and can't handle correction. Then we have the adult whose friends tell him it's okay to cheat on his wife, and he happens to love a TV sitcom about a husband and wife sleeping with any and every one. He doesn't notice that what he once considered cheatable offenses, he now excuses and looks at as acceptable. I can attest to this—that influence does take place—

from my own personal experiences. When I listen to music with a lot of profanity and messages of treating women like objects, I cuss more and view women differently. When I watch TV shows or movies that glorify sex and violence, I desire sex more and become callous toward violence. Our minds are sponges and absorb what we hear and see. Like food that is bad for us and gets the label of junk food, the garbage we see and hear is easy to access and permeates throughout our culture.

Being conscious of what's feeding our minds has never been more important. We can't bank on our culture and society giving us the essential lessons and ingredients to help us grow and develop for the better. We also can't lie to ourselves and say, "Oh well, it doesn't have any impact on me; it's just entertainment." We have to look in the mirror and KNOW it has an effect on us for the worse. On the other hand, we can feed our minds fruits for our growth. Those fruits being love, self-control, peace, and compassion, just to name a few. This gives us the chance to have positive self-talk and visualization theaters in our mind. This takes intention; this leads to growth. Reading books, studying history, watching documentaries, listening to podcasts and positive music, and associating with high-character people, and other outlets promoting the fruits for growth should be deliberately "eaten." Garbage or junk food can't be eliminated completely. The food pyramid recommends junk be limited for our bodies, and it's no different with our minds.

It's imperative to know what's influencing our thoughts. Our thoughts dictate our lives. What we see and hear creates our thoughts. Our thoughts dictate our feelings and behaviors. Our feelings and behaviors give us vision and purpose. Our vision and purpose drive our actions. Our actions dictate who we are and how we treat others and ourselves. How we treat others and ourselves is how we have impact and influence. Everything starts with a thought.

1. What garbage in your life do you need to eliminate?
2. What effects have you noticed personally from hearing or seeing junk?
3. What can the garbage you identified in number 1 be replaced with? List a replacement for each piece that can be eliminated.

"Everyone wants the cake, but few are willing to put in the time to let it bake." #ChampTalk

Cakes Take Time

Cake batter CANNOT be put in the microwave and then taste like grandma's special recipe. Time, love, and patience are the central ingredients for making a cake that can melt in someone's mouth. Why can't we grasp this concept when it comes to other facets of our life, like the areas we want to be experts in, skills we want to develop, investments we have made, and careers we are pursuing?

We want immediate results, and technology has cheated the process and brainwashed us to think that areas which will take a great deal of time are stupid and not really progressing since the results we want don't happen right away. Trouble and doubt arise when the results we want are not noticed, acknowledged, or occurring at the speed we'd like. This trouble and doubt stems from our inability to remain patient and persistent. Society wants us to feel we should have it our way NOW, and if it doesn't make life easier, then is doesn't make sense. Easier doesn't always mean better, and NOW doesn't always mean best. We realize it would not be smart to take a cake out of the oven early. We know doubling the temperature the directions say for making a cake and cutting the cooking time in half will NOT work. We know applying frosting right away when the cake first gets out and hasn't cooled is disastrous. We aren't surprised when a cake tastes awful because we switched ingredients. You nor I can name an amazing cake that was cooked in the microwave. That being said, we are conditioned by society and, at times, are enamored by shortcuts, quick fix schemes, and plans to cheat the process. We know the best cakes take time and specific steps, just like many factors in life. I can't imagine the entire process of making a cake is fun and intriguing. I know baking a cake can be time consuming and tedious. Great cakes take prep time, precise execution of directions, and a well-functioning oven set at the proper time and temperature.

We all want the cake. We want to be great in some form or fashion. The struggle comes with having the patience and restraint to discipline ourselves to train to become an honor roll student, a loving spouse and parent, an extraordinary leader, a successful business owner, or a beloved entertainer. Being great takes time, conscious effort and focus, following of steps, and patience. We can't become disconnected when we don't receive instant gratification. We can't lose vision of what we are really trying to do or want. We have to have hope and imagine how good the cake is going to taste when it is done the right way.

1. What is something you want to happen, which you find yourself getting impatient with?
2. What is something that took way longer than you would have liked but ended up being best?

"Pain isn't an enemy; it's more like an honest friend. Failure isn't an angry woman; it's more like a mother telling you how to win."
#ChampTalk

Honest Friend & Mother

As humans, we try to avoid pain as much as we can. Pain is inevitable. We cannot AVOID all painful situations in life. Pain serves as a great indicator to change behaviors. For all that, it would be mind-blowing for people to be able to explain all of the painful events in their life. Sometimes, we don't know why the pain is occurring or where it is even coming from. What can make matters even worse is when we do not use painful situations as learning opportunities or chances to grow. Pain communicates to us what we should do differently. **Pain is sometimes the only voice which gets our attention and tells us what we need to hear.** It is an indispensable lesson for toddlers to feel the pain of too much heat when they reach their hands close to a fire. The pain of the heat screams at toddlers to stop reaching toward the fire, and it is obvious the toddlers listen because they pull their hands back. They may not be able to explain it or understand, but the pain they feel causes them to change their behavior. Correspondingly, there are people who experience pain repeatedly but ignore the message to change because the pain is bearable. They choose not to listen, or they don't hear pain's messages until it's too late. The parable below gives a lesson on the danger of not hearing pain's message.

PARABLE

There was a little girl named Claudia, who was 11 years old. Claudia had a rare condition where her nerves would not allow her to feel pain. Most would think this is a pretty cool feature to have, but this ability to not feel pain caught up to Claudia. Claudia would fall, sometimes touch extremely hot objects, and even broke a couple of fingers, but she never cried or experienced pain. Claudia was seen as amazing to her friends and held in high regard, as if she was a superhero. Claudia's parents always worried for her and told her to be extremely careful on flaunting what Claudia considered to be a gift and a superhero trait. Like all young children, she began to feel invincible, and the praise she was getting from her friends boosted her ego even more. One day, when Claudia and several of her friends were outside playing they could see an electrical wire had fallen to the ground. Like most kids, they went to investigate. While investigating, a squirrel attempted to do the same thing. The squirrel appeared to be zapped by the wire, which was obviously live. The kids thought this was hilarious and then pressured Claudia to grab the wire. She loved the opportunity to wow her friends. She first put the back of her hand on the wire. Her hair stood up, and her eyes became huge; her whole body stiffened up, and the kids roared with laughter from the sight. She felt no pain. The attention propelled her to grab the wire and put on a bigger show. Again, she felt no pain, but the live wire caused her hand to clench around its end, preventing her from letting go. The other kids saw this wasn't her usual performance because she stopped breathing. They became terrified and attempted to get help; however, it was too late, and Claudia had stopped breathing before help could arrive. No pain caused this little girl to lose her life and feel indestructible. Feeling indestructible is one of the most deadly beliefs a person can ever possess. Pain is the one gift this girl never had to bless her to grow.

Comparably, failure is annoying yet essential. We feel failure can get her point across in a better way, or we flat out think the point she is trying to get across is irrelevant and pointless. Failure is NOT an angry or indignant woman though; failure is there to teach us like a loving mother would and always desires to do for her children. Good mothers want the best for their children, even though children don't always feel this way when a mother says "no" or doesn't give in to the children's demands. This is the equivalent to failure leading us to a number of possible avenues. These are avenues we needed to stumble across to actually progress. Failure is a phenomenon we try to avoid way too often. No one who has ever become someone worth talking about has avoided failure completely. The famous Coach K of Duke didn't even make the NCAA tournament until his 9th year of coaching, and in his first 8 years, 4 of those were losing seasons. Arguably the most known woman in America, Oprah, was fired from an anchor position early in her career and, on top of that, had to pay her dues before becoming a household name. A lot of times winners have failed more than losers; the only difference is losers fail and then give up. Failure is a great teacher and gives us lessons of humility, perseverance, dedication, and determination.

This is what failure actually teaches us and does for us:

A. Want to find out if you really love what you are going for? Failure can redirect you to your real purpose. Failure brings this out. Until I went a season without winning a game (0-24, if I remember correctly), I didn't really know if I just loved winning or if I loved the grind and other intricacies of coaching. *"No discipline seems pleasant at the time, but painful. Later on, however, it produces a harvest of righteousness and peace for those who have been trained by it." (Hebrews 12:11 NIV)*

B. We learn to enjoy or at least appreciate the process of achieving a goal or trying to get better at a particular task when we fail. **Believe it or not, sometimes in life, we need to lose. We need to fail and have hard times. We need it because it makes winning and success so much sweeter.**

C. We learn failure does not define us. We are not a failure just because we failed. Instead, we can see failure as part of the learning process, and usually there is something we have gained, whether it is knowledge, resilience, or an understanding of what it takes to be better.

D. Failure shows what was done wrong and, more importantly, what needs to improve.

E. Failure forces evaluation and questioning. Failure makes us ponder and wonder, "Is it really worth it to us?" Failure looks at the journey and asks the question, "Is the process being cheated, and is the dedication there wholeheartedly?"

Once I learned that 1 door closing means another door opening, an obstacle became a chance to get stronger. When God said, "Wait," it was because He wanted me to date a woman named Great, so I never looked at failure or adversity the same. #ChampTalk

1. *List 3 painful events in your life. What do you think you learned from each event?*
2. *What is something you failed at, and what did the failure teach you about yourself?*
3. *What are you afraid to fail at and why?*

17

"They say you learn from your mistakes, but a wise individual learns from another person's mistakes instead." #ChampTalk

Be Wise

The secret is not to look at another person's mistake to judge, boost our own morale, or find a new hot topic. Being aware of another person's mistake gives us a chance to study where he or she went wrong and apply what we have learned to our own personal decision-making applications. When we truly study one's mistake, we investigate and analyze the situation; this is a process where we examine the 'why,' the false hope, and understand where a person went wrong while figuring out how we can steer clear of similar offenses. This is why it is critical to have mentors and surround ourselves with wise people who have been there and done that. There is really no excuse to not learn from another person's mistake because there are so many information outlets dedicated to educating and enlightening us. There are people, books, television shows, documentaries, magazines, newspaper articles, YouTube videos, DVDs, and podcasts dedicated to sharing knowledge on human errors and where people went wrong.

Just from a curious and humble standpoint, I try to look at mistakes I don't feel one bit vulnerable to and just examine where a person went wrong. How does a coach close his eyes to allowing his program to be run like a mobster or mafia establishment? I bet most coaches who fell victim to this behavior thought just like me at a time and told themselves they would never close their eyes to evil. How about the burdening fact which troubles the heart of America when trusted adult professionals have sexual or inappropriate relationships with students? I would guess most adults who chose to go down this path didn't see it coming either and would take it back in a heartbeat. How about the alarming fact of how many marriages end due to infidelity? The average person who takes their wedding vows doesn't plan on cheating or see it in their foreseeable future; nevertheless, we know it happens every day. What makes this even more intriguing is if we look at the teachers, coaches, and spouses who fell guilty to these wrongdoings repeatedly. We will see nice, conventional human beings. We can and should learn from these mistakes, or we become susceptible to repeating them or falling desolate to our own demons we all battle with.

Now, from the confident "I can't believe someone would do such a horrible action" side, it is easy to judge and look down on people who have fallen guilty of indulging in these interactions. Conversely, there are other weaknesses and temptations all of us battle. There are monsters inside each one of us wanting to come out. For some of us, it may be breaking the law and justifying it because we think it should be legal. For others, it's not telling the whole truth, cutting corners, or fudging numbers. Personally, I've gotten in trouble with feeling invincible or as if some rules don't apply to me. One of the 7 deadly sins (gluttony, lust, greed, sloth, wrath, envy, or pride) wants to make us a slave to it and, at times, has had its way with us. We know this is true because we have all found ourselves saying, "I can't believe I did that" or "I don't know how I became that person" at one time or another. I know I have done and participated in some extremely appalling activities because I felt invincible, didn't think I'd get caught, and didn't learn from another person's mistake. I must admit, my mistakes cost me financially, stole valuable time, and humiliated me. Arrogance and looking at others saying *that will never happen to me* makes us feel invincible, and this false security leads to stupid misbehaviors, if we are not conscious of our own struggles.

We are all susceptible to some form of idiotic behavior, even as "normal" people. We can all be great, and we are all capable of angelic-type actions. In spite of this, we must realize even the devil was an angel. It all starts with a thought, and the thought can manifest if we do not admit it is a flaw and identify its ability to spread. From doing this, I have come up with a code of conduct anyone can and should apply. I will use the story of King David, who cheated with a woman who was married and then masterminded a cover-up to try and make himself look like a saint.

1. Examine "small" mistakes, thoughts, and feelings because what we deem as small faults, especially ones we think we are getting away with or no one will ever see, lead to BIG mistakes. *The first mistake King David made was not fulfilling his duty of leading his army into battle; he stayed home and sent someone else. The next mistake King David made was when he was on his rooftop and happened to see this gorgeous*

21

woman name Bathsheba bathing. Instead of turning his head from this naked woman, he watched and allowed his imagination to run wild. Before he knew it, he was doing research on Bathsheba and trying to figure out how he could admire her beauty in person.

2. You can't flirt with temptation or think, *I'll be stronger putting myself in this situation and getting out of it.* It is flat out dumb for an alcoholic attempting to stop drinking to go to a bar with his old drinking pals and think that is a good test for him to see where he is at. King David flirted with temptation by sending messengers to get this beautiful woman to come to him. On top of this, he knew she was lonely and would be attracted to him and his power. He flirted with temptation and probably used his status and position of power to convince this woman to cross the line with him.

3. Know who are you are and, more importantly, who you want to be. "Be disciplined to who you are because before you realize it, who you were, is not who you are…" King David knew he wanted to be a king who did what was right. He wanted the people to admire and stand for what was right. He forgot this in the midst of going after this woman and had committed an affair that led to the woman becoming pregnant.

4. If you can't tell your boss, family members, significant other, or would feel uncomfortable going in front of a church or huge company to explain your actions then it is something you

should avoid. King David not wanting anyone to find out about his affair should have been a sign to him. But wait, it gets worse. King David definitely didn't want people knowing Bathsheba was pregnant by him. This was obvious because King David planned a cover-up. King David summoned her husband, who was at war, to come back home. King David got the husband drunk, hoping he would want to have sex with his wife which would then make the husband look like the father. This didn't work because the husband felt horrible about being back home while his brothers in war were still on the battlefield. King David then created a Plan B and had the husband killed in battle. He then took Bathsheba to be his wife, and he looked like the kind king taking a poor widow into his home.

5. This may be the hardest concept to do—but step outside of yourself and give the situation you are in advice, as though you are speaking to someone else. King David didn't want to admit his mistakes until he took himself out of the equation and just looked at the big picture. King David was tricked into giving himself advice. A prophet visited King David and gave him a situation where David began to realize he had participated in some heinous acts. The prophet told David this story…

There were two men: one was rich and the other poor. The rich man had a ton of sheep and cows, while the poor man had only one little female lamb he had bought and cared for like it was his child.

The rich man had a visitor come to him who was hungry and wanted him to prepare food for him. Preparing food for visitors was a custom in their culture. Even though the rich man had many sheep and cows, he took the poor man's lamb and prepared it for the visitor. King David was irate hearing about the rich man and even said the rich man who did this certainly deserves to die. King David then added the rich man should pay back four times the price of the lamb since he did this without a care or any pity for the poor man. What makes this so unique is the prophet Nathan was describing King David. King David was the rich man. King David had not taken a lamb though, he had taken another man's wife and then had him killed to cover up a pregnancy from their infidelity. If King David would have never viewed this situation from another person's viewpoint, he would have kept making excuses or justifying his egregious behavior.

We all have made mistakes. We could have all avoided mistakes if we studied those ahead of us too. Wisdom is available to anyone who can learn from another person's mistakes to make sound judgements and avoid unnecessary distress to one's mind, body, soul, and character.

"Nothing beats a failure but a try is a lie because a half effort try is like a blind open eye." #ChampTalk

Blind Open Eye

The phrase, "Nothing beats a failure but a try" is overused and is interpreted wrong by people majority of the time. In today's world, it is often the wrong idea to sell since so many people think if they're out there giving *some* type of effort that is good enough. Trying when aiming for excellence is about giving the absolute best we possibly can, and if we fail then we fail; therefore, the phrase, "Nothing beats a failure but a try" is justifiable and carries some weight. The person who goes out and gives marginal effort and looks at everyone and says, "Oh well, I tried," is not being realistic with himself or herself. At times, we are afraid of giving our absolute best and failing, and that is a normal fear each of us may face. Great coaches, smart CEOs, and successful entrepreneurs would not classify these as valid attempts, if the effort and focus needed was not committed to procure excellence. After years of coaching, I have noticed my definition of TRYING differs greatly from my young players' definitions of playing hard and TRYING. *Coach, I ran when you said sprint.* A lot of times, I give athletes a time limit on how fast they should do the required running. Some athletes have to give their all to make the time, while others can coast to make the time with ease. My question to the athlete who coasted would be, "Was that as fast as you could run?" to get them to see they could have done it in 2 or 3 seconds less? *Coach, I went for the rebound.* Sure, they went toward the ball, but I would challenge them by asking, "Did you dive on the floor when the opportunity presented itself for you to actually get the rebound?" *Coach, I tried to play defense*, but the question is, "Did you finish the play, slide over to take the charge and willingly sacrifice your body or move out of the way?" *Coach, I came to practice today and tried*, but "Did you give your best effort and focus to each play and each drill?" Not to mention, if you don't prepare you can't try your best. A player who chose to stay up too late and chose to not eat and drink properly before practice can't give maximal effort and focus. In similar fashion, I've had students who said they've tried. *I gave my all and still failed the math test.* I do some digging and find out they studied for only 30 minutes the day before the test. I then ask them how much time and what steps they believe they would need to take to get a perfect score and not just pass the test. Based off the information they give me, I break down to them that truly trying would be studying for 30 to 60 minutes 3-4 days in advance by doing actual problems, finding someone to review steps they seem to be struggling with, and completing all homework prior to the test. My job is for them to see there's a difference between giving minimum effort and maximum effort.

In essence, how many people fully immerse themselves into a particular task and don't fear failure? The answer to that question is: not a lot. We have been brainwashed to think if we fail, we will continue to flounder in future attempts. We are missing the point. What we must apprehend is those who are great at something have failed many times. The Wright Brothers, who were the first to fly a plane, failed dozens of times; however, unlike their competition, they never gave up. They learned the invaluable skill of picking themselves back up and continued trying persistently to reach the heights they envisioned themselves reaching.

If you're going to try something, you need to give it the lionhearted preparation, focus, and effort to be great. Otherwise, it is like having eyes but not being able to see anything. Looking does not equate to seeing, and trying does not equate to success. If you are blind and looking, you definitely will not see, and if you are giving half effort, you definitely will not reach your full potential.

1. What is something you do that you have not been giving maximum effort and focus to?

"A man who sees discipline as a restraint to his freedom is a man who will ultimately limit and rob himself many freedoms of life."
#ChampTalk

No Discipline, No Freedom

The definition of discipline, according to Oxford Living Dictionary is, "The practice of training people to obey rules or a code of behavior." In some form or fashion, *we are all disciplined* by something in life. There are so many athletic, talented, smart, beautiful people who never come close to reaching their potential in sports, school, their career, life, and so on. The big question everyone always asks is: Why didn't they make it? The answer in most cases but a few is simple and sad—they lacked self-discipline in a significant area. It's beyond monumental to choose what you are allowing to discipline yourself because how you train is how you will act unconsciously and what you will resort to in the toughest situations.

The aptitude to have vision separates the self-disciplined from the undisciplined. When you can see the big picture, play a trick in your mind, or constantly remind yourself, it will be worth it, this is special and separating. If you want to be great at something, then you must have great discipline. Pick your disciplines wisely and know not picking one is still choosing one. Let me break this down some. If I say I won't be disciplined to eat all vegetables or attempt to train my body to only eat certain foods: all this means is I'm disciplining my body to eat anything. Another example which comes to mind is when people say they will not be conditioned to believe in any religion or any god. Believing in nothing is still a belief in something. If people are not disciplined or, as some might say, "conditioned" by a religion, a book like the Bible, or a philosophy, that just means people have created a god of their own liking.

Too often people look at discipline as the losing of freedom. Here is an awesome point I heard Charles Stanley, Gary Vaynerchuk, and Tony Robbins make on separate occasions. This point brings everything to light. Their message was, "The reason you have [financial] freedom is because of the times you've had [financial] discipline." Without the discipline to save, work, budget, and make investments, you will never have [financial] freedom, and instead you are disciplining yourself to be broke. There is no way a person can have freedom with ANY and EVERYTHING; you can't have freedom without having discipline. The more discipline you have the more freedom you will possess, and the more freedom you have the greater the discipline is needed.

1 Corinthians 10:23
[23]"'I have the right to do anything,' you say—but not everything is beneficial. 'I have the right to do anything'—but not everything is constructive."

1. **List at least 3 freedoms you desire to have. Next to each desire list the discipline each freedom requires. Then come up with a way to maintain that discipline.**

Below are some examples of how discipline and freedom go hand in hand:

- *An athlete who disciplines herself to be in excellent condition has more freedom to play with a great deal of energy and has a lower chance of experiencing fatigue in her competitions.*
- *A student who disciplines himself to study for an hour each day has more freedom to answer questions with wisdom and knowledge.*
- *A husband who disciplines himself to show and demonstrate he loves his wife has more freedom to grow and find joys in marriage.*
- *A woman who disciplines herself not to do drugs or drink alcohol has more freedom to make sound decisions without an added negative influence.*
- *A self-employed carpenter who has disciplined himself to treat every job as though it is his own earns the freedom to pick from a number of jobs.*

"Embrace the moment, grasp the challenge, and reach for the future." #ChampTalk

Embrace, Grasp, Reach

We all have difficult trials to face in life. Regardless of the misfortunes, we can embrace them and grasp the chance to expand ourselves as human beings. You don't have to believe everything in the Bible, like I do, or even anything in the Bible, to appreciate the story of Joseph and his numerous obstacles and major setbacks. Joseph is such an incredible example of embracing the moment and grasping the challenge, and that allowed him to reach for the future.

The story of Joseph goes something like this: first he was thrown into slavery and shipped to a foreign country because his brothers were extremely jealous of their father's favoritism toward him. The brothers sold Joseph into slavery to get rid of him. Most people would have allowed being sold into slavery to ruin them. On the contrary, Joseph embraced this challenge and worked as a noble slave; he made the most of this situation. Joseph earned the trust of his master to the point of running his master's entire household and being entrusted with everything he owned. Just when it seemed like everything was looking up for Joseph, his master's wife tried to seduce Joseph to get him to have sex with her. What did Joseph do with this challenge? He embraced it and took the RIGHT course of action instead of the EASY course of action. The easy course would have been to sleep with his master's wife and brush everything under the rug. This didn't go well for Joseph because the upset wife yelled rape and got him thrown into prison (for doing the right thing)! Joseph was left with yet another obstacle. Instead of whining, complaining, and feeling sorry for himself, Joseph embraced being in prison. He saw prison-time as an opportunity to grow, and still did his best. While in prison, Joseph gained the trust of the prison guards and was respected by all the prisoners there because of his character and wisdom. A couple of prisoners who wanted their dreams interpreted came to Joseph with questions. Joseph was not bitter or an example of the motto, "misery loves company"; he interpreted each of their dreams and shared the news to the prisoners that one of them would soon be free and restored to his original position of working under the Pharaoh as a cupbearer. Joseph didn't ask for money or fame for sharing with the prisoner what his dream was about. Joseph only asked that the prisoner, Pharaoh's cupbearer, would remember him. Joseph asked that the cupbearer remember him by telling Pharaoh about Joseph being unjustly in prison. The prisoner who was restored to his position of cupbearer did remember Joseph—two years later though!

Joseph is an unbelievable example of embracing the moment and grasping the different challenges in front of him, instead of running or shutting down. Since Joseph always embraced the challenges, he eventually ended up being second-in-command, only behind Pharaoh, in a time where Egypt was the number one world power. Joseph saved the entire country of Egypt and many other countries. Though it took Joseph over 13 years and some major rock-bottom moments to reach this position, his ability to grow and find positives make him a beautiful illustration of how you can only reach for the future and meet your full potential when you embrace every moment and grasp each challenge, regardless of how tough it may be.

Who in their right mind would have looked at being thrown into slavery, separated from ALL family and friends, falsely accused of rape, and imprisoned for years for doing the right thing as great opportunities to make the most out of their future?! I don't know if anyone could say yes to this, but as seen through the story of Joseph, if a challenge is there, running and feeling sorry for yourself does NO GOOD. There is always something to learn, an opportunity to grow, and an appreciation to be instilled through moments of turmoil. If we don't learn and grow from the pain and heartaches, we have wasted time and opportunities. How we respond is the key. We don't have to understand what is going on every moment to trust in the fact that we have the ability to learn from hard circumstances; the appreciation of these hardships may come later on down the road. Look at Joseph, I'm sure he didn't understand why he was having all these tribulations. Although 15 years or so later, while he was second-in-command, sitting on a throne and saving an entire continent, I know Joseph could look back and appreciate how he had responded to events earlier in life. *If there was no pain we'd never grow, kind of like if there was no rain, grass would never show.*

Challenges are there to help us grow, believe that!
If you're going to go out, go out swinging. If you're going to feel pressure, create diamonds. If you're going to settle, settle for excellence. #ChampTalk

2 Corinthians 4:8-9 New International Version (NIV) [8]"We are hard pressed on every side, but not crushed; perplexed, but not in despair; [9]persecuted, but not abandoned; struck down, but not destroyed."

Questions to ponder and think about:

1. Can you identify a time you chose the wrong route? What influenced you to take this route?
2. When obstacles are many, how do you make the most out of those tough situations? Identify or create your own personal steps, views to take, and messages to tell yourself.
3. Having optimism, good character, toughness, and patience are needed to give yourself a chance at fighting through tough times; when did you lack this? How do you think things could have been different, if you had shown these traits?

"Boys push down the trash, but men take out the garbage." #ChampTalk

Take Out the Trash

A few roommates I lived with in college constantly added garbage to a packed trash can by pushing it down when it was already full, or they would put the trash next to the garbage can. They claimed they didn't have "enough time" to take the trash out. I was jokingly made the father of the house because I was the most responsible. I had a choice to make: ignore the problem or take out the trash. I couldn't stand the smell or the look, so I stepped up and took out the trash repeatedly. It took more time to clean up the area around the garbage can, not to mention sometimes going through the hassle to double bag the trash. The time could be cut in half at least, if the trash was taken out when it needed to be. Oh yeah, and it would have prevented the house from smelling like old Ramen Noodles, onions, and warm hot dog water on a hot summer day!

This quote represents so many different issues in life. We are in a culture where people do not want to take care of problems or situations right then and there. On a lot of occasions, it wouldn't even become a problem or situation if it was taken care of promptly and responsibly. Sadly, we are in an era where people would rather wait for the next person to deal with the issue instead of taking care of it themselves. We have to fight off the feeling to push off or procrastinate matters of life until another day or until someone else comes along and does the job. This is exactly how some individuals let their lives become and wonder why they are so stressed or *all of a sudden* these bad things start to occur. These issues have been building up over time and have been calling for attention in a subtle and quiet fashion.

It's pretty simple but definitely not easy—constantly look at yourself and the decisions you are or are not making. **Handling business immediately is the answer. If you can do something today, don't push it off until tomorrow. Tomorrow the task will only be greater, and you'll have initiated the habit of *putting it off*,** also known as PROCRASTINATION.

1. Are there any tasks you are avoiding, which will only continue to get larger and worse? If so, what are they?
2. In what areas do you wait for someone else to step up and take the lead, BUT you could step up instead?

"The ability to succeed is limited to the willingness of one to sacrifice." #ChampTalk

Success Requires Sacrifice

The more success one desires usually means the more one must sacrifice in order to achieve that goal. The big factor and where people lose focus or don't drive themselves to sacrifice is due to their lack of vision. Many desire success. At the same time, so few are willing to put in the work because they are terrified of the journey. The path to greatness is narrow, while the path to destruction is wide.

Being around sports my entire life, either through playing or coaching, has given me the opportunity to see what true sacrifice means. I hear so many adolescents say, "I want to be a professional basketball player" or "I want to be in the NFL." They swear up and down they really, really want this to happen. Nevertheless, few are able to sacrifice and find the time to hone their craft to even give themselves a shot at this ridiculously hard challenge. Most experts say you need thousands of hours of good, focused practice to become a master at a particular craft. They give me excuses, such as they didn't have access to a gym, were busy with homework, had to work, had a party to attend, didn't have the right equipment, were a little under the weather, and the list could go on because I have heard it all. By no means am I saying there are no other important facets to life, but there are 24 hours in a day. Time waits for no one, and there is a choice we all make on how we are going to use our 24 hours each day. Sacrifice doesn't mean giving up something one doesn't care much about. True sacrifice is giving up that fun event, foregoing the easy and simplistic way, surrendering immediate pleasures and comfort, and forfeiting enjoyable but toxic relationships. When people make sacrifices they are slaughtering immediate pleasures as an offering to greater fulfillment.

I have seen someone first-handedly REALLY want success. The success he wanted was to be a Division 1 football player and the best possible football player he could be. Kevin Zeitler, an all-pro guard who played for the Cincinnati Bengals before going to the Cleveland Browns and becoming the highest paid guard in NFL history at this time, WANTED to be the best football player he could be. Some would argue he was extremely talented and was a natural born athlete, but he wasn't. He was not some natural precocious phenomenon. Having seen him play in grade school, he didn't stand out. He wasn't the best player on the team. He wasn't even the best or most feared at his position. When he got to high school though, he had something more important than talent. What Kevin did have that made him scary and special was a body which could handle the grind and punishment (he didn't break down) and a drive and will to match it. This allowed him to commit to bettering himself each and every day and develop his skills. This man transformed his body from being a chubby, slow, out of shape kid into an impressive physique comparable to a comic book superhero. This wasn't just a wish or goal. This was a commitment he made for his lifestyle starting in high school. I considered myself to have a great work ethic and commitment to getting better in football, but when I saw Kevin's commitment and training, he was on an entirely different level. If you want to marry success you have to be willing to date "hard work." He made a commitment to work out every day in terms of weight training, flexibility, film study, and diet and nutrition. Not to mention, there would be days where he'd do two workouts/weightlifting sessions. A session could last up to 2 hours. Kevin prioritized and sacrificed the immediate pleasures of parties, social media attention, more sleep, junk food, drugs, and alcohol to put himself in a position for the ultimate success. His talent and skills grew but were not what made him stand out. His unique drive and will combined with the fact that his body didn't break down are what make him remarkable. People who really want success in something will understand immediate pleasures can't come before the commitment to hard work and striving to get better.

1. What is something you want to do or to have, which you know requires a lot of sacrifice? List 5 different sacrifices you could make to give it a chance.
2. What are you NOT willing to sacrifice that is holding you back?
3. What are some of the hardest sacrifices you have had to make?

41

"Most people don't want to have the truth for free; they would rather be a sold dream they can't afford." #ChampTalk

How Much Do Dreams Cost?

What if I told you, you could have a mansion with a huge backyard, a pool with a Jacuzzi, a maid, any type of car you want, a bank account which saw at least seven zeros, and you didn't have to do much work for it? Most likely you would tell me this is too good to be true, and you know what, this is too good to be true! People often chase dreams but don't give a lot to make them come true, and there are people who prey on individuals who believe they can get this dream for a limited cost. Those who prey on these people sell them the dream and make light of the hard work, dedication, commitment, and unavoidable struggles necessary to achieve success. Ironically, there are some predators who prey on these individuals because they honestly don't know any better themselves, while there are some predators who see the prey as a great monetary or ego boost come-up for themselves.

The line to be sold a dream is very long. Be that as it may, dreams cost a great fortune and, figuratively speaking, make many go bankrupt. Often times, prospective insurance salesmen are sold a dream plan for success. Who doesn't want a quick $100k to make a

43

few phone calls to sell insurance everyone needs as much as they need to drink water or to breathe? It sounds sweet! They leave out the fact that there's a great chance you will fail. They leave out the part about working 12 hours a day, making 50 phone calls or emails (cold-call style at that), and how you'll have to bend the truth.

I can't count how many parents have gotten taken advantage of because they have this idea and dream of their child receiving an athletic scholarship, playing a Division 1 sport, and then becoming a pro. They spend tens of thousands of dollars sending little Timmy to exposure camps and tournaments across the United States. We are taught to chase exposure and attention from coaches. We do not realize that, when seen by a college scout, we're only going to be exposing an average or maybe even bad product and a mediocre Little Timmy who belongs nowhere near a Division 1 stadium, complex, or facility unless he's attending as a fan. It's tough to hear the truth that we have to spend thousands of hours, at a minimum usually, to become great at a particular task, career, or skill. We don't want to be told we can spend 10,000 hours and still not achieve that sexy, amazing dream we've always wanted. If the dream deals with making a ton of money or being famous, it can require even more sacrifice and unique abilities. We don't want to hear we don't have what it takes. Parents don't want to hear they have screwed their kids over in the genetic lottery. We don't want to face the fact that we haven't put in enough time and hard work. It's easier to blame someone else and not face the cold hard truth of, "I'm not good enough" or "I don't have what it takes." You just might not be designed to do it.

Now some may be wondering about the success stories of all the superstars who seem to come out of thin air or make it, despite the naysayers. "Look at Aaron Rodgers or Russell Westbrook! They came out of nowhere. No one knew their talent." A lot of Division 1 universities might not have given these guys much attention while they were in high school; however, these type of superstars—who seem to come out of nowhere—have remarkable talent, incredible athleticism, size (in a lot of cases), and an "it" factor that can't be denied over time. This is why professional athletes can come from Division 2 and even Division 3 colleges. People love to hear the stories of how a player or person like that came out of nowhere, although they miss all of the pivotal facts and factors, which can't be taught or developed without this wonderful thing called being blessed or lucky.

Some scream, "Anything is possible with God," but this doesn't mean God makes EVERYTHING possible for each person. Even if you don't believe in God, it is beyond obvious that we each have unique skills, gifts, talents, and abilities. Each of us has a path to follow or skills and talents that can be maximized more than others. I'm going to give you the truth and this is for free: **you can be anything you want is a lie, but you can be something great if you try.** Knowing and understanding your purpose is more important than chasing what seems to yield money and fame. I have to have more than a WANT in order for something to happen. I have to have a number of cards in my hand to make it come true. Reality is free, but we don't want it when it gives us the answer we aren't looking for. The sad thing is, WE ALL NEED REALITY AND MUST FACE IT SOONER RATHER THAN LATER.

"A goal without a commitment is a wish, and last I checked none of us have a genie."
#ChampTalk

Genies Don't Exist

Almost any type of self-help book looks at making or creating goals and the importance of having an end goal in mind. Very rarely do they tell the candid truth that goals, even really well thought-out and attainable ones, are not **guaranteed** to happen just because you made it a goal. If you don't have commitments you can follow, then your goals were not carefully constructed. *I want to be a neurosurgeon. I want to be a mechanical engineer. I want to be a professional athlete. I want to be a veterinarian.* Ok, what commitments are you going to make to achieve this distinct goal you have in mind? Each of these goals is attainable, yet they are nearly impossible to achieve if an individual does not put a set of commitments in place and then HONOR those commitments. Commitments are in a person's control, unlike a lot of results we chase or strive for. A wise commitment focuses on improvement and reaching excellence. Individuals know they have committed to the right thing, if it is something they can do within their control and gives them a great chance to improve. I'm going to list a few different goals all over the board, so you can get an idea of worthwhile commitments. The below commitments work towards a goal and give people a shot at fulfilling that goal:

Goal: Average 20 points a game (basketball)
Commitments needed to be made:
1. I will make at least 100 3-pointers, 100 finish moves, and 100 free throws each day of the week in the summer.
2. I will watch at least 10 minutes of film each day in the season.
3. I will go for every backside offensive rebound I can in the game.
4. I will do 10 minutes of visualization on particular moves/skills and slow methodical practice after each practice.

There is no way a person can control how many points they score—some nights another teammate may have more opportunities to score, the coach may diagram a game plan where the player needs to be more of a facilitator or screener, or, at times, the ball just doesn't find the basket. The goal is copacetic, but the bigger objective should be to become the best possible player one can be. We are infatuated with numbers and love statistics. What if the player scores 20 points shooting 25% (which is a horrible percentage for those who don't know basketball) or what if the player has an opportunity to score 30 points but only gets his original goal of 20? Having a goal is not wrong, but we have to be honest with ourselves and aim to be the best we can, rather than being consumed with numbers or statistics. When the opportunity arises, it is all about doing the best you possibly can.

The decisions made on how to allocate time, energy, and focus (through commitments made consciously or not) can push someone to the next level more consistently than a goal can.

Goal: Get accepted and attend an Ivy League school

Commitments needed to be made:

1. Read a book at least once a month that focuses on the major the prospective student is thinking about studying or that will help with personal growth or expose the student to different ways of pursuing excellence.
2. Spend at least 20 minutes each day in the summer looking at ACT/SAT prep material and/or vocabulary words.
3. Contact and research admission offices of at least 10 different schools to see if there are summer programs to attend to increase chances of getting accepted.

When looking at something where you have to be accepted, some of the control is out of our hands, especially if a committee is looking for a particular characteristic you cannot possess such as race, gender, socioeconomic status, and location. These uncontrollable characteristics can be criteria for some acceptances. We can't control those influences, but if you want to be at your best when the opening is there, wise commitments being practiced give you the best chance at attaining the goal. Wise commitments can be controlled, focus on consistency, and are geared toward improvement.

Goal: Lose _____ lbs. and get more toned or muscular.

Commitments needed to be made:

1. Eat breakfast, lunch, and dinner. Snacks are okay but must be fruit, vegetables, or nuts. Eliminate fast food, fried foods, candy, chips, and desserts. 1 cheat day allowed.
2. Only drink milk or water—1 day allowed for juice, soda, or alcohol.
3. Go workout at least 30 minutes, 3 days a week, for 3 months straight.
4. Research and create 5 different 30 min workouts you can do at your home, gym, or outside, so there are no excuses (3 focus on cardio and 2 on muscular strength and endurance). There are great apps you can download to help out with this.

This is a goal for the average person for sure. Some people have no clue on how to go about making this goal become a reality. This may be one where people have the most control but struggle to stay committed because of all the temptations. It's tough because there are both diet and exercise components. Another tough part is breaking bad habits. Without a doubt, the most grueling part which defeats the average person is due to the fact that it is a long process, and there is only delayed gratification. You might do the above commitments and see very little gain in a week. We can't forget that a little gain is still a gain, and this is a slow, tedious, and mentally strenuous process.

If you don't have commitments to go along with your goals, then you have yourself a wish list. Just wishing doesn't get it done. Wishing takes no responsibility. Wishing does NOT prepare for the big moment, it only hopes for it. Wishing expects a genie to perform a miracle; to no one's surprise, genies aren't for sale or I have yet to be fortunate enough to run into one.

Take note that all of the above goals had realistic commitments. The commitments focused on consistency and were not just large numbers. Although, the bigger the goal, the bigger the commitment should be. If a high school player is looking to be an all-conference performer or play in college, then he or she may want to be making around 500 shots each day at the very least in the offseason. Notice the basketball commitment didn't have a crazy number like make 5000 3-pointers in a day. If the commitment is too demanding that can be really frustrating and cause stress. The stress will then lead to quitting. The weight loss commitment didn't have a workout time of 2 or 3 hours; it gave a time that is manageable but still fruitful. Of course, there will be days where you dread meeting that commitment, but if it's attainable, you can hold yourself to a higher standard and not allow for excuses. In like manner, there will be days you feel motivated and will go above the commitment minimum, and that is part of the reason for using the phrase "at least" with a lot of the commitments. Consistency is the chief principle in making this work.

Remember: the bigger the goal, the more consistency and days needed for the commitments. Instant gratification is not your friend; delayed gratification is.

1. List 3 different goals you have.
2. Create 4 different commitments for each one that help in achieving that goal. Think about the time, repetitions, days,

and/or steps needed to give yourself a chance at achieving that goal.

3. Post these goals and commitments in a place where you are reminded each day. Find someone to share your goals and commitments with. Choose someone who will help hold you accountable.

"Your all is your all, and 100% is your all." #ChampTalk

110% Isn't Real

Those who know me understand my annoyance with people claiming they are going to give a 110%. I understand why people say this, but there are so many **concepts** wrong with this thought. The "extra" 10% we feel we are giving is really what we are capable of doing. We can't give more than 100%. Energy, effort, preparation, and focus are consistently the criteria on whether the 100% bar is met. 100% should be our pure focus, and getting to that level is hard in and of itself. Just because we completed a task or got the job done doesn't mean we gave a 100% either. Identically, at times we lie to ourselves and think we can make up for missed opportunities or times where we didn't give 100%, and the fact of the matter is that we can never MAKE UP what has been lost; it is lost, gone forever, and never coming back. Having said that, we may do better or might have enough time to seize the opportunity the next time. Even so, time waits for no one. Great coaches, trainers, teachers, bosses, and special people challenge us to give 100% and not settle for just getting the job done. They grasp the fact that each opportunity and "time" is a unique blessing presented to us to help us grow, learn, and build character. The more we can be cognizant that trying or giving 100%

53

allows for us to reap the most benefits, the better chance we have in becoming the best versions of ourselves.

1. What do you need to give 100% to?

"A fool puts trust in himself to find money and success, but even money will tell you how to get more money and find success: In God we trust." #ChampTalk

Money Has a Secret

"The only person you can trust is yourself," is what some will say and firmly believe. The themes that permeate society are: stay focused on the goal and do whatever is necessary to make it to the top. Money is one of the measurements we use to determine success in our society. Money is equated with the ability to live comfortably and freely. To be TRULY SUCCESSFUL, one must trust in someone even greater than his or herself. A dollar bill has a slogan and idea that could make anyone TRULY SUCCESSFUL, and the message a dollar bill suggests is to trust in the almighty God.

The quote below sums up everything in a nutshell:

"A fool puts trust in himself to find money and success, but even money will tell you how to get more money and find success: *In God we trust.*" #ChampTalk

There is a Source (God) who knows us better than we know ourselves. If some of us had a bunch of money, it would lead to a downfall or be the epitome of us squandering our purposes and placing the meaning of life only in material possessions. Likewise, when we know our purpose (trust in God) and realize there is a plan for us—a specific plan for us—it gives us a peace and satisfaction hard to imagine. To add to this, once we realize God may want to use us in a special or specific way, it becomes a lot easier to accept the situations or circumstances which do or do not happen. Patience, trust, and hope are key. Solomon, in the Bible, is one of the greatest examples of showing patience, trust, and hope in God and truly understanding his success could only be achieved through finding his purpose.

Before looking at Solomon, I want you to think about what you would ask for if you could have ANYTHING, and it could actually be yours without any crazy catch. Some would pick health, some would pick love, but most would pick money or something that deals with money. Instead of Solomon asking for a bunch of money when God asked him this exact question, he displayed his trust in God by asking for something that would please and honor God. He asked for wisdom to become a better man, a better king, a better father, and most of all a better servant to the Lord. Solomon trusted God to give him what he needed most for his special roles. Solomon saw his purpose, and he changed his focus to serving, honoring, and leading his people first because being a king was a unique yet burdensome role God had given him. Even if you do not believe in God, you can look at Solomon and see he had a greater purpose than to please himself. When we examine the life of Solomon, we come to see that Solomon had a time where the only person he focused on and tried to please was himself. In spite of that, he still felt empty. He still was miserable, and he came to the realization that all the stuff in the world could never fill his need or define him as a person. He had tons of money, beautiful women, different palaces, lots of gold, too much jewelry, and the ultimate lavish life of a king. In possessing it all, he realized it was **meaningless** without purpose; he didn't have success. Solomon was at his best and most successful when his selfishness was replaced with selflessness—when he was rooted in his foundation and asking himself the question of what is my purpose in life, and who can I trust to give me this purpose? Solomon was most preeminent when he realized his mission was to lead his people and put them first. What is your purpose and what is your mission in life? If you haven't discovered it already, *Purpose Driven Life* by Rick Warren is a good book to help guide you in finding your purpose.

Solomon's ability to take his selfishness out of the equation and think about his entire nation is an exemplary attitude that can be modeled and shows us in order to leave the greatest legacy possible, find the most success, and be remembered for ages, you have to be willing to have a greater purpose than to please yourself. When Solomon understood the importance of his mission—to be a king— he desired to be a servant leader who found trust in a greater plan and source outside of himself. Solomon understood it was better to trust in God. He desired to fulfill his heavenly Father's purpose and was rewarded by being a great counselor, leader, and writer AND, on top of that, one of the richest and most prestigious kings ever. **Matthew 6:33 "But seek first His kingdom and His righteousness, and all these things will be given to you as well."**

1. If you could have anything in the world, what would it be? Does it serve others, if so how?

2. Some of the questions I've asked myself to find my purpose and what I want to do in life have been:

    a. What would I like to do if I didn't get paid for it?

    b. Who have been some of the greatest influences in my life?

    c. How can I best love, serve, and invest in others while finding enjoyment in doing this?

3. Based off these questions, what do you think your purpose in life is?

4. What actions and situations do you put others' well-being first?

"Time is not meant to be found; time is meant to be made." #ChampTalk

Time Can't Be Found

Time is, without a doubt, the most important entity. Unlike money, fame, popularity, status, and feelings, if we lose it, we can't get it back. Too many do not value time and realize it is up to them on how they spend their time. The amount of time we put into something gives it value and shows how much we truly appreciate that relationship, craft, or job. You don't find time to be a neurosurgeon; you don't find time to be a master architect; you don't find time to be a Hall of Fame athlete; you don't find time to be a loving and caring parent; and you don't find time to be a compassionate spouse—you must MAKE time.

It was easy to lie to myself and say, "I don't have enough time." Despite that, we constantly prioritize how we use our time—some of us do it subconsciously and others consciously. **If you look at how you spend your time, you truly see what in your life you find most valuable.** When you feel pressed for time, especially, and might be under stress, look at how you spend your time during those high-pressure moments. You will see what you truly value. Look at what you choose to do in those pressing moments where you say, "I have no time."

I found myself in this trap, thinking I valued my faith and development most as a man, but I was not spending nearly as much time in those areas as I did, compared to other *stuff*. I decided there were some things I needed to limit or eliminate altogether. I didn't cut out positive things I valued, like my health, fitness, relationships, or coaching. I cut out or limited the *stuff* like TV, music, social media, and going out. I struggle daily with this balance. Regardless, by being self-aware, I am better able to put what I value ahead of all other distractions. Distractions *waste* my time rather than *make* my time valuable. I started reading more books. I began listening to podcasts and sermons. One of the beauties I found is I could be smarter with my time, and I could kill two birds with one stone in regard to certain things. For instance, I realized I could be on the elliptical, not just working out but also listening to podcasts, sermons, or TED Talks instead of music. I could also listen to knowledge-based outlets while I drove, got ready in the morning, or prepared for bed (shower and teeth-brushing time). Similarly, I made a conscious effort to see my friends and mentors for dinner, lunch, or to just sit down to pick their brains and build relationships where I could discuss my faith and absorb wisdom on how I could become the man I strive to be. I didn't realize I was doing this, but in college, I found I could fill two needs with one deed by inviting and having friends come workout with me. It has gone from inviting friends to workout with me to setting up open gyms where we get together and play basketball on occasions. I get to work on my fitness and build relationships at the same time.

Previously, I described some positive ways I have been able to multitask; despite that, multitasking can be dangerous. A lot of matters in life will get done faster and more efficiently, if our undivided attention is given. I don't multitask well when I'm trying to parallel park into a tight spot; I save myself from multiple attempts and my success rate goes up dramatically when I turn off the radio or get off the phone because my focus is improved and distractions are eliminated. In the same way, when I was in the process of writing this book or even trying to create a practice plan or lesson plan, I discovered I work best when the TV is off, no one is talking to me, and my phone is to the side. I went from taking an hour to do a lesson plan or practice plan when the TV was on to doing it in 15 minutes. In return, this gave me more time to sleep or do a different task. Relationships and effective communication aren't fans of negative multitasking either. Text messaging while someone is attempting to talk to you doesn't make the person giving you the message happy. When we don't give people our undivided attention, this can flat out prevent us from understanding what someone else is telling us or cause us to take much longer to process it. We waste time and energy. Although multitasking is beneficial at times, there are lots of tasks which need our sole focus and can be done more efficiently when we give it our sole focus.

Whatever you value and want in life, you must make time for it. There is *always* something to distract us and take our time away. There is always that thing we say we don't value or care about at all, trying to climb up our priority list and steal from our time log. If you keep saying, "I have to find time to do _____," I'll tell you this now—you won't *find* the time. The only way something

61

is going to change is if you start *making* the time, putting what you really value at the top of your priority list and planning everything else around it.

1. What do you SAY you value most in life? List the Top 5 things. Who do you value most in life? List at least the Top 3 people.
2. What are you spending your time on, which you should cut or eliminate? List at least 3.
    a. When you work out, get ready in the morning, or travel to your destination, what are you listening to?
    b. How much screen time (technology) do you have outside of work or school?
    c. How much sleep and get ready time do you need?
    d. How much spiritual, intellectual, and physical development do you take each day?
3. What needs to be given more time in your life? List 3 things, at least. Explain how you will give more time to each one. Can you multitask and do any of them together?
4. What, in your life, needs more time but would be completed faster and more efficiently if you did NOT try to do it while multitasking?

Example 1: **This person wants to increase professional development and physical development.** This person spends 5 hours a week watching different television shows. Instead, he will watch only two hours per week. When he does watch TV, it will be when he is working out. For the other 3 hours, he will read articles or books to help in his professional development.

Example 2: **This person wants to spend more time with his wife, improve his work performance, and make more time for his spiritual development.** Right now, he spends 8-10 hours a week playing video games, being on social media, and watching sports on television. Since he has an hour commute to work, he will listen to different devotions in the car. He decided he will complete his work first, delete the apps off his phone, make Wednesday a date night for his wife, and limit his video game play to only a couple of hours on the weekends.

"It's hard not to judge a book by its cover, so I try to read as many books as I can."
#ChampTalk

Book Covers Aren't Enough

Judging a book quickly and by its cover and judging people swiftly and based off their looks correlates strongly. Getting to know another person and hearing a person's story can help us grow, since the message or story may uniquely speak to our heart. This is exactly why certain people are placed in our lives at certain times. Race, height, physical stature, body type, clothing, and whether we find a person attractive or not play a role in a hypothesis we all create when we see or meet new people. These judgements we make about people are shaped by our own personal experiences, as well as what the media constantly portrays with their messages in television, movies, news reports, and music.

We all judge, and I have become very conscious of some of the judgments I make due to a person's physical appearance or first impression. Since I am aware of my prejudices, my curiosity motivates me to get to know a person on more than a surface level. It has become part of my DNA to desire to get to know people and find out what makes them tick or just who they are as a person.

Judgements, especially when they are negative, cause individuals to put down a book which could have a positive influence and help them grow. Listen to their story and read their "book" with fresh eyes. I have been wrong; physical appearances do not tell each and every story in an articulate fashion. Read as many books as you can. The genuine authenticity often times offered in getting to know people beyond their outward influence can change both sides. The key to life is relationships, and the key to knowledge and wisdom is reading. Reading books along with people are life changing antidotes to hatred and self-absorption.

1. How are you judged based off your appearance?
2. Has a judgment made by others because of your appearance ever been wrong? How did this misjudgment affect the relationship?
3. When have you recently judged someone by their appearance? How are you going to take the time out to get to know the person?
4. Who is someone you misjudged based off a first impression or appearance?

"Move in a way where they don't hear your steps but can see your footprints." #ChampTalk

Move in Silence

Our culture is all about getting noticed, getting exposure, getting seen, and getting what we deserve. It seems like the loudest mouths get heard the most. When someone hears our steps, we are definitely going to get noticed, but when we leave footprints, that's a mark of real influence that can last. Have you ever seen someone stomping around to be noticed? The noise gets people's attention, and attention, more times than not, is more important to the person stomping around than the actual effect.

There is a difference between marketing and gasconading. What do you think about the guy on Facebook who posts he's going to go volunteer and feed the hungry? That is awesome, right? Even so, too many times and we start to question his motivation for posting it. If it's to inspire or encourage more people to come then, by all means, do it, BUT if it's to put himself on a pedestal and say, "Look at how well I'm helping someone out" then save it. I know some of you are thinking in certain cases you have to make that noise and get attention. Nonetheless, what I want you to see is, if your focus and concentration is on making noise and being seen, then your attention is not on

@ChampionLife23

inscribing your brand of excellence. **The issue is not in the fact of being seen, getting attention, or making noise. The issue is when all of those factors keep us from making an impact, a lasting impression, or actually doing something that will stick.** What's more important: *to tell others what you're going to do or to actually do it, to be heard or to be listened to, to be noticed or to be respected?* Some can stomp and make imprints, more power to them. Be that as it may, we can never forget the imprint is why we remember them.

In the same way, a person who is braggadocios is going to miss a lot of opportunities to learn, make a difference, and leave people wondering for the better. It's always a sign of a person's character when the place they left is better afterward because of their presence. This is a footprint. Those especially who are really humble and genuine have an opportunity to get put on pedestals, like no other in view simply because they are so self-effacing.

Remember: there's no point in being noticed or heard, if no one can even remember what you said or did positively.

1. Is there something you wish you got more credit for but seems to go unnoticed?
2. When have you been more concerned about getting noticed and not about making an imprint?

"No one can be a better you than you, and no one can be a better me than me." #ChampTalk

One You

If you've ever been in the process of "replacing someone," and you happen to be after someone who was just talk and had no influence, you don't have to worry about being compared to that person negatively. In contrast, there is a reason why great people are often feared and deemed as tough to follow. They leave massive impressions. It's always a sign of a person's influence when the place they left is better after because of their presence; this is a sign of excellence. The beauty is though, a great person might have left an awesome impression; however, we definitely shouldn't and don't need to walk in their shadow when we can create our own, one-of-a-kind shadow.

We've been lied to. The goal shouldn't be about being better than him or her. The commitment should be to be better than the last version of ourselves. My junior year in high school, I digested this lesson quickly. Arguably, the best running back to have ever played at my high school graduated, and I was up next to be the featured running back. Despite having similar builds, my coach often reminded me I wasn't as fast or explosive as him, and this was true. I

@ChampionLife23

could not be him, and I did not try. My focus was just to be me, get better each day and see what would happen. I learned and did incorporate skills and traits from the previous running back that fit me. My mission was to maximize my strengths and improve my weaknesses, instead of trying to be the next someone else. It panned out pretty well, winning back-to-back state championships. What was surprising to me is how some would mention my name as one of the high school's great running backs, sometimes ahead of the running back before me. From a statistical and talent perspective, he was without a doubt better. Still, what I learned is some appreciated a different style and factored in intangibles. There will always be those people who we can never please, while there will always be those people who love us for us. We usually can't please them all. I would have robbed myself of enjoyment and growth trying to be a better someone else.

Correspondingly, we're encouraged to compare instead of appreciate. Who's better between Aaron Rodgers and Tom Brady, more impactful between Martin Luther King Jr. and President Obama, and more important between Oprah Winfrey and Barbara Walters? They're all special and unrepeatable people. Each one we can learn something from, even learn to the point that we can take a skill or trait from them and shape it to fit with who we are. Discover differences and unique characteristics to appreciate; every single one of us possesses them. We CAN control being better than an older version of ourselves. We CAN'T control being better than someone else.

"Too many are infatuated with being better than the next person, instead of being better than their last." #ChampTalk

1. When you compare yourself to others, is it to learn from them or to be better than them?
2. When competition is removed from the equation, what can you learn from others' work ethic?
3. When is a time you just focused on improving yourself? Do you feel like you made an improvement? Were you satisfied with the results?
4. Is it more productive to compare yourself and your efforts to others competitively or to consider how the successes of someone else can contribute to your well-being?
5. Which is more important: competition or collaboration? Why?

"I would rather take time to help build a beautiful home right than to take time to repair one built wrong." #ChampTalk

Building vs. Repairing

A home constructed the right way by being built on a solid foundation provides the ability to withstand and remain on the course through different attacks and challenges. Being in the real estate and landlord business, I know building or constructing a property the right way and not falling in love with quick fixes is the best route. When getting a place, I'll spend maybe a month or two longer compared to my counterparts who just want to rent it out quickly. This may be two months of rent I have to pay, but my time spent repairing, dealing with angry tenants, and having to work around someone else's schedule is minuscule or not an issue at all. If the message to adhere to more importantly is, "I just need to get done as quickly as I can, even if that means taking shortcuts," you're guaranteed to have more problems and repairs needed OR more times than not, you'll have to just start all over because the quick fix is a quick break. This will cost you more money and time, and continuously add to your to-do list. I don't have time for fixing a bunch, and I'm sure you don't either, so focusing on

@ChampionLife23

doing it right the first time and making sure everything is exemplary and upright is critical.

In similar fashion, it takes long spans of exerted energy, persistent preaching, demanding, and only allowing the best behaviors when constructing a project, starting a business, coaching a team, developing a blueprint, raising kids, or building an actual home. A plan that hammered out the "what ifs" is not going to have the same struggles or future repairs compared to another plan quickly thrown together or that just decided to *wing it* on the fly. A home built on a sturdy foundation of good principles and promotion of high character makes sure every step was followed to the tee. This takes more time but eliminates so many complications down the road versus a home built on sand, quickly done and rushed through. Plus, there's also a special sentiment and appreciation you have when building or creating a foundation of excellence and knowing it can endure the storms of life.

1. What are some areas or skills in life you wish had a more rock solid foundation?
2. Do you have a sturdy foundation in the areas which matter the most to you in your life?

I created a list of 4 areas in my life.
- Education: *This wasn't my doing, but my parents would read to me and with me. Also, they'd do flashcards with me and encourage me to read as much as possible when I was younger. Along with this, my dad practiced math facts a ton with me, so my foundation had a solid base.*

- Coaching/Teaching: *Read books, allow other coaches to mentor me, attend clinics, study film, and most importantly work at a school with the same philosophy of caring about the character more than test scores and winning.*
- Relationships/Family: *I try to make time to see how they are doing by scheduling dinners, text messaging, planning and attending gatherings, and supporting them as much as I can. I try to let them know they are loved and appreciated. Keeping in touch is a focus.*
- Finances: *Research and find people who are good with their money and in a similar position as me. Create a budget and track spending. Have different ways to save and make money, stay as debt free as possible, and don't buy it if it's out of my budget.*

List ways for each point in regard to how you will and/or have created a solid foundation of excellence:

- _____

- _____

- _____

- _____

- _____

"Sometimes we sacrifice the loving and wise person we desire to be, in order to give people who we think they deserve." #ChampTalk

They Deserve...

How many times have you had someone disrespect you, do something completely dumb, or treat you like less than a human being? In those situations, we're encouraged by our human nature to retaliate with harsh or condescending words and actions. It's natural to have the philosophy of an eye for an eye and a tooth for a tooth.

Some of us have been taught to hit the switch and give them exactly what they deserve, which is a case of verbal fire and whatever else it takes to get our point across. We all want to stand up for ourselves, and fight fire with fire. In those times especially, we have a decision to make on whether or not we are going to stoop to that person's level or take the high road and give them what they don't deserve. It's natural to feel they don't deserve love, kindness, and respect. *I'll be nice to you, if you allow me to be* is really an excuse though. The main time to be loving and kind to people is when they're obviously going through things or are in a negative state. When you are conscious and want to be a more loving, pleasant person who is wise and positive in the way you conduct yourself, you're then faced with choices.

"Be disciplined to who you want to become because before you realize it, who you were is not who you are…"

He cheats on you, so you slash his tires. Your co-worker bad-mouths you, so you bad-mouth her when you get the chance. Someone says something so stupid and ignorant that you look at him with disgust and counter the stupid remark with a stupid comment of your own and give him the middle finger. Don't get this confused with me saying you shouldn't stand up for yourself OR just stop interacting with that person at all; I'm saying, don't become them. We can always express discontentment of how we are being treated in a smooth way. It's not easy, but it's definitely possible; it's absolutely a must if we don't want to forfeit the potential we have to become a better person—a person who is WARM-HEARTED, POSITIVE, and OPTIMISTIC. I look at it like this: the only way we can get even with an ugly person is to become ugly, and unfortunately, ugliness has lingering effects. All of a sudden, we're not the person we desired to be. We're a monster who has lost control and may start lashing out at innocent victims.

Remember, fire enjoys more fire. If we want to be a better, more sagacious and positive person, we have to forgive those who haven't even asked or whom we feel don't deserve our forgiveness. Forgive, respect, and grow wiser, so you can embrace who you are, appreciate who you're not, and love who you are becoming.

Proverbs 15:1 "A gentle answer turns away wrath, but a harsh word stirs up anger."

1. When a person lashes out at you, what is your default way to address the problem and confrontation?

2. When is a time you lashed out on an innocent bystander because that is your default go-to?

3. Have you ever engaged with someone and got just as rude as them or even taken it to the next level? How could you have handled the same situation in a kind and polite but firm manner?

4. When is a time you stood up for yourself in a kind and polite but firm manner?

"When you believe in your mission, it is easy to preach with all your heart." #ChampTalk

Mission Driven

I learned a valuable lesson while coaching boys' basketball at the middle school level because I was really challenged with my philosophy I was teaching the kids. The philosophy some challenged, was the man-to-man defense I believed in. Though this was not the NBA and I wasn't making a fortune doing this, I gained great insight. I was faced with a situation where we had lost to a team twice. The first time was by 20 points, and the second time by seven. Parents and players questioned the philosophy, mission, and the system I had put in place because of the losses. This was tough and is something every leader—whether in business, sports, or education—is faced with when the results are not "winning." Second-guessing is natural, if IT doesn't work right away. Now I'm faced with the situation, do I abandon my philosophy or mission? Am I just being stubborn? I had to see which one was the reason for why I was going to stick with man-to-man. I evaluated the situation, and I made the decision to keep our man-to-man defensive system with the feeling this system would give us the best opportunity to get better and the best chance to reach our potential. My reasoning for this was: 1) playing man-to-man defense would provide the most opportunities for them to truly learn the game of basketball and reach their potential, 2) it would take too much teaching time to put in an effective zone, and 3) there wasn't enough time to do this. So, I stuck with my guns and stayed the course. I added wrinkles to what we were doing. Sure enough, we got another opportunity to face this team in the championship of the biggest tournament. This was the third time we played them, and we were down by nine right away, looking like we were about to get blown out. I called a timeout so everyone could hear the message I believed in. I was very calm, and in my heart, I still thought we would win. My players would not have bought into or believed in the system if I showed any sign of doubt in what I was telling them. Long story short, we were able to make a major comeback. My team was very poised, calm, and never got flustered no matter what adversity struck during that game. That's when I realized the players believed in the message I was preaching and had the identity I wanted them to have all season. The identity I wanted them to have was to take charges, sacrifice, move fast on the court, remain tough, and, most of all, never panic.

I realized from that situation, changing your philosophy or wrinkling it is not always an abandonment of your true philosophy. Sometimes you do have to evaluate, constantly reflect and ask yourself, "Why am I doing what am I doing?" OR "Why am I teaching what I am teaching?" If you can't give a reason or justify it, then change should be made. More importantly, you have to be willing to stay the course and be okay losing or failing the early battles to give yourself an opportunity to have a shot at winning the war and allowing your training to rise to the occasion in the most stressful and crucial moments. All this was highlighted from coaching a boy's middle school basketball team!

"It is a lot harder to move from excuses to success then it is from failure to success." #ChampTalk

1. When is a time someone wanted you to abandon or reconsider your way of doing something? What did you do?

2. When challenged, can you explain or justify the reason behind why you did or are doing what you did/do?

3. How have you made something better because of someone challenging you?

"You only get change back when you give more ... literally and figuratively." #ChampTalk

Change Back

She walked up to the cashier and gave the man a hundred-dollar bill for a $.75 candy bar. It's very apparent she wanted a bunch of change back. How we get change seems like such an easy concept our society frequently glances over and doesn't apply enough to situations outside of money. If people want to get better at a particular skill, trade, or practice, they need to give more. If gurus want to become more knowledgeable and wise, they need to give more. More is what is needed to see change. What that "more" is depends on the change desired to be gained. More could be a greater attention to detail, an increased time commitment, further service given, a choice to love, a bigger demand in effort, a substantial extent of patience, a rise in researching, a considerable jump in stick-to-it-ness, etc. Giving more in one or more of the above areas is how to get the change needed.

Sometimes, the only more we need is *more time*. In other instances, it's not just more time but also a greater focus and an increase in effort. There are reasons we limit the change we get back though. We underestimate the cost and try to do just enough to get by. We forget to factor in the taxes. We expect the cashier to cut us a break. The greater the cause and the higher the cost, the harder it is to get change. There will be and are uncomfortable times when the price tag is not visible. We then have a choice: we can hope and wish we have enough or prepare and make sure we have more than enough. The cashier of life can't keep our change, so it's better to give more and eliminate the chance of regret than to be S.O.L., embarrassed, and not have enough.

1. What is something you underestimated the cost it would take to see a change? How could you have given more looking back at that situation?
2. What change would you like to see in your life? What more can you do to ensure it occurs?

"Great ideas are like checks: you need to cash them to claim their true value, and you must do so while the funds are present." #ChampTalk

Cash the Idea

Every year, unique and awesome ideas are put into practice. There are always new inventions, new businesses, new approaches, and new ways to do things. They become innovations that change the way we live our lives, view the world, and go about our everyday duties. What we don't realize about a lot of ideas is that they are NOT singular visions or thoughts; they are actually owned and possessed by numerous people. Still, the person who puts the idea into practice and makes it come to fruition is often times looked at as the originator or the great mind who thought like no one else. This is not the case though, when you really look at the overall view. I know people who had the exact same idea as Uber or Lyft 10-15 years ago. I've heard people discuss the idea of creating an app which carries video footage and shows people exactly how to perform certain weight training exercises, and now that exists. I've seen people make bold predictions on which companies will skyrocket to the top and be awesome investments, and they were right. The sad thing about it is none of these awe-inspiring ideas were acted upon by the people I'm referring to. If you have a great idea and you think you are the only person in the entire world with that idea, chances are you are highly wrong. Now, it doesn't matter if you are or aren't the first person with the brilliant idea, but it does matter significantly if you're the first person to act and make this grand idea a reality and not just a thought. It's like these special seeds are in their possession but never have a chance to bloom in their garden. Then, the seeds get discovered by someone else who then plants them elsewhere, and they bloom.

People, every day, have great ideas but do nothing about them. Some don't have enough vision and are pessimists, so they make excuses and complain why it won't work. These are the types of people who have an awesome idea but find all the reasons for why they can't make it happen and play the victim role. Subsequently, there are people who convince themselves they have to keep all the return, glory, and money for themselves. This group of individuals hoard the idea when they really need others to help. These people ultimately end up with nothing because they won't allow someone else to help the idea become a reality. Then there are those who are clueless on the next steps to take and DON'T research at all. Next, there are those who don't write down the idea or get consumed by every day duties and just don't make the time to develop the idea into a plan. Last but not least, there are those who are afraid to risk hardships and failure with their idea, so they do absolutely nothing but say, "I knew that was going to be big!"

Ideas are like checks, and checks only show their true value when they are cashed. Great ideas are meant to be found and want to be cashed. This is the equivalent to an idea having a meaningful impact when it is actually put into play. The average person can come up with a great idea, but a plucky person will do everything in his/her power to make the idea become a reality. Every idea might not be great, or a person may fail in making the thought into an actuality, but what I can promise you is if it is a great idea—a check worth cashing—you better believe the idea is going to find someone who will turn it into an innovative reality. This person could be you, if you're willing to go cash the check.

1. What are some ideas you had that have now come to life? What was your reason for not acting on the idea you had?

2. What are some ideas you have NOW and think will eventually come to life? How are you going to act on these ideas?

"Sometimes people get so frustrated by locks on doors that they never even check to see if the door is already unlocked." #ChampTalk

Check the Door

Sometimes doors have arduous locks, and everyone knows locks require keys or some type of combination. Doors can be intimidating, massive, and complicated. I'll be the first to admit, even though I have a door with two sets of locks, I don't always lock my doors, especially when I am expecting company. Sometimes, I just flat out forget to lock the door. It always makes me chuckle a little bit when I have people banging on the door or ringing my doorbell like a maniac, but they never even checked to see if the door was open. Now I guess some would say it's rude to just walk into another person's home, but if the person has a "Please Enter" sign on the door, some will see the sign while others will still only see the locks. The expectations an individual possesses makes all the difference. When I have people who know I am expecting them to come over, they usually check to see if the door is open. This relates to someone who has an optimistic viewpoint when approaching new or different situations, challenges, or opportunities.

@ChampionLife23

The fact of the matter is, there are three possible answers to going up to the door and checking to see if it is locked or not. First, the door is open because of one of these possibilities: A) someone is expecting you, B) there's an open door policy and walk-ins are welcome, or C) someone forgot to lock the door. Two, you ring the doorbell or knock, and someone eventually opens it up. Three, you go up to the door, ring the doorbell and knock on the door, but there is no answer (the door stays closed).

This corresponds strongly with the fact that most relationships, jobs, and opportunities we desire have a door in front of them waiting to be opened. Although, there are times the "locks" (tasks, challenges, and obstacles) are NOT really the thing holding us back—instead, what is really holding us back is ourselves. We can psyche ourselves out and come up with a list of reasons why we CANNOT open the door. Our state of mind begins relating to our thoughts of feeling incapable or hesitant to attempt particular tasks or jobs and to our attempt at opening the door. Our mind and our belief can move mountains, OR it can build doors with strenuous locks.

1. Name a time you shied away from an opportunity without even attempting to see if it could happen.
2. What doors in life seem to be the most intimidating and have the most locks for you?
3. What is the first thing you see when you're in a situation? Is it the door and opportunity, or is it locks and obstacles?

Thoughts to ponder next time you meet a big door with locks and an obstacle:

- Look for the reasons you should attempt to seize the opportunity instead of reasons for why you shouldn't even try:
    - Check for "PLEASE ENTER" signs, doorbells, and the lights being on.
    - Check to see if the door is open. Be sure to knock, and ring the doorbell.

"Too many ask to walk on water but don't even go to the shore." #ChampTalk

Walk On Water

To give ourselves a chance at miracles, amazing things, or the impossible to happen to us, we must at least do our part. If we want to walk on water, we have to at least be willing to go to the shore. A man walking on water is one of those things that seems preposterous. If you do not know the story I'm alluding to, I'll sum it up for you rather quickly. Peter, who was one of Jesus' main followers (called the 12 disciples), did the unthinkable and got out of his boat at sea and walked on water one night in the middle of a storm. When you look at the historical account of Peter, there are a number of steps Peter took to allow the inconceivable to occur. Any person can learn from Peter's steps. First, Peter was at least in a place where there was water: he was in a boat. He could not attempt to walk on water if he was in a desert or in a location that did not have a hint of water. Next, he took a chance in taking a step. The rest was up to God, a higher power or whatever you want to call it. The point is NOT that God needs our help or that someone is going to do everything for us because then we'd be robots, and there would be no fun in that. If Peter didn't do his part, there wouldn't have been an exhibit of faith; there wouldn't have been a demonstration of hope that anything is possible, and impossible is nothing at times. The third thing we see from Peter is how he ignored the wind and waves of the storm when he decided to step onto the water. Peter ignoring the wind and waves is like a person ignoring the naysayers, doubters, haters, and pessimists (who often call themselves "realists"). Peter had a focus on what he really wanted. When your focus is on the right thing, don't be shocked when things start to fall into place or the impossible becomes possible. Now, don't get this twisted and think the impossible will always happen simply because you put yourself in the position or because you attempt it. I can tell you though that **if you do nothing** and don't even get to a place where there is a chance for the inconceivable to happen, you have no chance and zero hope of doing the unremarkable. At least walk to the shore, and see if a voice tells you to "come."

1. Make a list of things in your life you'd like to have happen but that seem extremely tough or even impossible.
2. From the list you created, what makes it so tough or seemingly impossible?
3. What are some actions you could take to make the above list have a chance of occurring, even if it's a slim chance?

**"When you truly LOVE someone or something, you love even when you don't <u>feel</u> like loving."
#ChampTalk**

Love Equals Action

PART I - Something

It is EASY to love something when we are extremely motivated, the process has just begun, and we're getting the feedback and results we want. Love is tested when we are in the middle of the process and can't see the finish line or big picture. It's tough to love when we are exhausted, irritable, annoyed, or unmotivated. True love, however, is displayed when we do not have the feeling of love present. Instead of being fueled by a feeling, we should be fueled by a fundamental belief. A belief that will shape and discipline our behavior when the feeling of *'I love this'* is hidden. The uncommon realize this feeling is gone momentarily, so they must force themselves to see the big picture, remember their dreams, and discipline themselves.

We have all likely heard the phrase, "Actions speak louder than words," so it should be no surprise when I tell you displaying love is not done through words but actions. When we truly love something, our energy, time, and effort goes in that direction—even when it is HARD to find that feeling of love at the given moment. What we often forget is the road to achieving greatness and actually displaying our love for something is best seen when the road is full of obstacles, our bodies are tired, and our minds are shooting off tons of doubts and questions asking, "Is this worth it?" Remember, we don't get any brownie points or kudos because we said we loved it. We ONLY get something out of it when we push and grind for what we love. It might be hard to picture, but Stephen Curry didn't relish every minute of training in becoming a perennial all-star and MVP, Shakespeare didn't enjoy every moment of creating masterpieces, and Dr. Ben Carson wasn't entertained by every book on his way to performing miraculous surgeries—YET, I can assure you, they took action for what they loved even when they did not feel like loving!

PART II - Someone

Now when it comes to loving some**one,** the philosophy is similar. It starts with one first understanding what it means to love someone though. Love is unconditional. One of the best definitions of love comes from the Bible. The Bible says, "Love is patient, love is kind and is not jealous; love does not brag and is not arrogant; love does not act unbecomingly; it does not seek its own, is not provoked, does not take into account a wrong suffered...Love never fails" (1 Corinthians 13: 4-8). Love is a commitment, despite flaws you are aware of and see.

Loving parents of newborn babies are awesome figures to emulate because they love their babies who are young, whiny, poopy, sleep-killers, even when they (the parents) are tired, stressed, and testy. Another group of people who make a covenant (which is greater than a contract) to love, even when they don't have the feeling, are married couples. Not to anyone's amazement though, the fact is the divorce rate is higher than ever in our society. I can imagine every man and woman has woken up and not had the feeling they once had for their significant other when they first got married. Yes, even happily married couples have experienced this before. I'm not talking about the lovey-dovey feeling being gone because of mental or physical abuse or because of someone cheating. I'm talking about the feeling of love missing because they've been married for 15 years, it's starting to get annoying because their significant other is unorganized, the couple doesn't have the same hobbies they once had, or the spark is not lit as brightly as it once was. The difference is, the divorced couple doesn't push through and one or both quit, ending the relationship in divorce. Yet, if they only realized love is so much more than a feeling; love is an option someone selects. So next time someone is a pain-in-the-butt, use it as a great opportunity to love them because our feelings won't want us to.

True love is a choice you make, especially when you do not FEEL like loving someone.

1. What are some of the reasons that make you want to NOT love something or someone?
2. List at least 3 things you say you love but are tough for you to love at times. Why is it tough to love? For each one, list an action you can take to love it better.
3. Who is someone you say you love but is tough to love at times? List an action you can take to love that person better.
4. List at least 2 things that need your love but that you have failed to love. For each one, list an action you can take to love it better.

5. List at least 2 people who need your love but whom you have failed to love. For each person, list an action you can take to love him/her better.

"Those who have a horse in the race always care more about the outcome." #ChampTalk

Get a Horse in the Race

There is a common detest with cancer that most people share with one another. With other issues in life, this common perspective can be quite difficult to find, due to location, culture, race, and experiences. My level of interest is a lot lower, the farther away an issue is from me. It's human nature. Hurricanes have plagued the southern coastal states in the United States. These hurricanes do not directly affect me. I do not live close to these areas. I did not have any property or assets damaged. I do not have close family members or friends who have been affected by these hurricanes. It's nearly impossible for me to care as much as a person who lost someone or something because of the hurricanes. I can't have the same emotion as someone who lives there and had property destroyed. My investment in caring comes from being an American who wants to empathize with other Americans. In the same light, there are hurricanes and catastrophes that happen in other places. I know little to nothing about these catastrophes, and I, honestly, have not shown any care or concern. In the world we live in, we are almost taught not to care, sympathize, or empathize with situations and events outside of "us." Additionally, society teaches if it does interfere and might even cost us money or power, then stay out of it and hold onto our "serenity."

A great illustration of people holding onto their power in America is displayed through racism and privilege. Racism is real in America. Racism empowers and gives privilege to some, while suppressing others and making some seem "less than." This may be hard for certain groups to admit, accepting they are not directly affected in a negative way. They do not have an investment or chance of repercussions because their personal experiences and relationships have not allowed them to be on the negative end of racism. Human nature pushes us to invest in what most likely impacts and changes our everyday life. A movement like 'Black Lives Matter' is likely to matter more to blacks than whites, given that blacks feel and know they have a higher likelihood of being racially profiled and harassed by the police. Prior experiences of being racially profiled make 'Black Lives Matter' a reality. At the school where I teach, we did a training for the faculty members which focused on race. One of the activities done by the presenter, Glenn E. Singleton, forced some to realize they didn't have a friend or even someone they could call to ask a few questions who happened to be another race. My white co-workers admitted there were issues they realized they had not cared about or given thought to because it had little to no impact on their lives. We came to a collective agreement that certain issues and problems didn't light a fire under them in the same way, since they did not feel like they had *a horse in the race.*

What we noticed was white teachers who had black friends or good connections with their black students, often were more

102

empathetic and cared about issues like white privilege, the current ramifications of slavery, and police brutality at a higher rate than those who didn't have a black friend or a good connection with their black students. If a white person happened to have a black son or daughter, they were even more aware and empathetic toward racism.

When we have someone we care about personally affected, it forces us to change our entire outlook. It might not be that people do not care, but it's hard to truly care or be invested if you are not directly affected. Ignorance is real. You don't know that you don't know at times. What's even worse is when we think we know, but we really don't know. **Additionally, at times, we don't want to have a horse in the race and place our comfort, enjoyment, pleasure, or peace on the line.** There is a major inner battle when one of these is put into question. Racism was so indisputable in the time of slavery. People of color were viewed as less than human beings—⅗ to be exact. The southern white slave owners put their comfort, enjoyment, pleasure, and peace above the slaves' lives. It is easy to cringe and wonder why the slave owners couldn't see slaves as human beings. The slave owners avoided having a connection to the slaves and instead connected to money, power, personal satisfaction, and prosperity. This connection took away their empathy. *Having a horse in the race* does cost us something; nevertheless, the chance to gain life-changing insight is worth it.

1. What are the dangers in not understanding or being empathetic to issues others have and/or complain about but don't personally affect you?
2. What are some issues you think you should be more aware

of and empathetic toward?

3. Do you have someone of a different race, culture, religion, socioeconomic status, or upbringing which you would feel comfortable having an in-depth conversation with? If you answered 'no,' what can you do to build relationships with others of this liking? If you answered 'yes,' how have those relationships changed your way of viewing the world?

Author's Answer

The Solution

100 years from now, where will America be?

Ask the same question a 100 years ago, and our tomorrow none would see.

Women say, "Don't trust a man," and maybe that's because of the average man's plan.

Kids desire to grow up fast; adults desire to live in the prime of their past.

Black or white, young or old, rich or poor, one world we hold—

Fame and fortune, power and glory, how much could one get for a soul sold?

The idea that money rules the world confuses those who are even younger.

What happened to looking out for your neighbor and making sure there's no hunger?

If you're doing fine, do you really have time to care?

Do you really have blessings to spare?

You need more. We need more. It doesn't matter that we can't take any of it to heaven's door.

A country built on God is the same country that rebukes God.

Education has become just a thought—a diploma is more like something you bought.
So where are we going? Where are we headed?
This self-seeking, lost world—I'll admit, I'm one of the many that fed it.
We can hope and dream for change, but we need more than everyone's two cents to gain.
Sacrifice and suffer now, and the sun will still shine in the rain.
The solution is complex yet so simple:
Love God, love others, and love yourself;
Look at the common bond of us being human as a reason to call all your brothers.

"People who worry about the pie miss out on the cake." #ChampTalk

Share the Pie

We all want to hold onto the slice of pie we have. Some have a bigger slice of pie than others. Human nature fears sharing will cause us not to have enough or to be "satisfied." Whereas, if we share our slice of pie and look at others as brothers and sisters—or even as human beings—we would, in most cases, end up getting some cake in return. We could have a smorgasbord of abundant returns, if we'd just share our pie.

Acknowledgments

Throughout my life, so many people have inspired me to write *#ChampTalk* because of the love, support, and care they have provided. Writing this book made me realize there are tons of people to thank. The list is endless. To my coaches, present and former athletes, present and former students, teachers, professors, pastors, friends, and family, I thank you.

Thank you to those who directly contributed to the process of creating this book. I have to thank my friend, Eric Wright, for creating a marvelous book cover and applaud him for bringing to life what I envisioned in my mind. I'd like to thank Asiah Gregory for creating the illustration in the book and Carolyn Sachs for putting her special touch on it and finalizing it. Maddie Bloomquist, one of my awesome students, I'd like to thank you for your commitment to being the first to read the book through and give me great feedback, unique perspective, and encouragement. Mason LaMarche, one of the hardest working student-athletes I have ever been around, I thank you for editing in the early stages and providing great wisdom. Thank you to my editor, Meloni Williams of D.O.P.E. Publishing, for your insightful feedback and guidance throughout the process; your advice and perspective was greatly appreciated and needed.

I want to especially thank all those who read this book and share it with someone you know it can inspire, challenge, or make appreciate the pitches life throws at us. We are all teachers and learners to someone, and I thank you for allowing this book to help you identify that and to make the most of those opportunities when you see them.

Last and certainly not least, I have to thank God. Thank You for the lessons you have given me along the way. Thank You for providing for and showing me what true love is through Jesus Christ.

Made in the USA
Monee, IL
05 April 2021

64859375R10073